TENNESSEE

The Volunteer State

BY
JOHN HAMILTON

Abdo & Daughters
An imprint of Abdo Publishing | abdopublishing.com

abdopublishing.com

Published by ABDO Publishing, a division of ABDO, PO Box 398166, Minneapolis, Minnesota 55439. Copyright © 2017 by Abdo Consulting Group, Inc. International copyrights reserved in all countries. No part of this book may be reproduced in any form without written permission from the publisher. ABDO & Daughters™ is a trademark and logo of ABDO Publishing.

Printed in the United States of America, North Mankato, Minnesota.
072016
092016

Editor: Sue Hamilton   **Contributing Editor:** Bridget O'Brien
Graphic Design: Sue Hamilton
Cover Art Direction: Candice Keimig   **Cover Photo Selection:** Neil Klinepier
Cover Photo: iStock
Interior Images: Alamy, AP, Dollywood, Dr. Macro, Dreamstime, Getty, Grand Ole Opry, Granger Collection, History in Full Color-Restoration/Colorization, Gunter Küchler, Hollywood Wax Museum, iStock, Leaf-Chronicle, Library of Congress, McClung Museum-Univ. of Tennessee, Memphis Grizzlies, Memphis International Airport/Walker Parking, Mile High Maps, Mountain High Maps, Nashville Predators, National Park Service, New York Public Library, Nissan Group of North America, Oak Ride National Laboratory, One Mile Up, Pinson Mounds State Archaeological Park, Sun Records Studio, Tennessee Titans, Titanic Museum, University of Tennessee, Vanderbilt University, Water Valley Casey Jones Railroad Museum, Wikimedia, & William Henry Huddle/Dallas Museum of Art.

Statistics: *State and City Populations*, U.S. Census Bureau, July 1, 2015 estimates; *Land and Water Area*, U.S. Census Bureau, 2010 Census, MAF/TIGER database; *State Temperature Extremes*, NOAA National Climatic Data Center; *Climatology and Average Annual Precipitation*, NOAA National Climatic Data Center, 1980-2015 statewide averages; *State Highest and Lowest Points*, NOAA National Geodetic Survey.

Websites: To learn more about the United States, visit booklinks.abdopublishing.com. These links are routinely monitored and updated to provide the most current information available.

Cataloging-in-Publication Data

Names: Hamilton, John, 1959- author.
Title: Tennessee / by John Hamilton.
Description: Minneapolis, MN : Abdo Publishing, [2017] | Series: The United
    States of America | Includes index.
Identifiers: LCCN 2015957732 | ISBN 9781680783452 (lib. bdg.) |
    ISBN 9781680774498 (ebook)
Subjects: LCSH: Tennessee--Juvenile literature.
Classification: DDC 976.8--dc23
LC record available at http://lccn.loc.gov/2015957732

CONTENTS

THE VOLUNTEER STATE

Tennessee is a land of many personalities tied together by its Southern culture. The three white stars on the state flag represent the Grand Divisions: three regions, each with its own rich heritage. The mountainous East is home to Great Smoky Mountains National Park, Appalachian crafts, and bluegrass music. Middle Tennessee has farms and country music. The West has cotton farms, the blues, and Graceland, Elvis Presley's beloved home.

Many Tennesseans live on farms, but there are also bustling cities filled with manufacturing businesses, music clubs, and BBQ shacks. There's always something to do in Tennessee, from the roar of a NASCAR race to the quiet solitude of fishing on a remote mountain lake.

Tennesseans are quick to lend a helping hand. During the War of 1812 (1812-1815) and the Mexican-American War (1846-1848), the government needed soldiers to fight. Thousands of Tennessee citizens volunteered for duty. That is why Tennessee is nicknamed "The Volunteer State."

Hundreds of stars perform at the Grand Ole Opry in Nashville, Tennessee, each year.

QUICK FACTS

Name: Tanasi was the name of a Cherokee Native American village. The name was later used to describe the Tennessee River, and later, the whole region.

State Capital: Nashville, population 654,610 (Nashville-Davidson County)

Date of Statehood: June 1, 1796 (16th state)

Population: 6,600,299 (17th-most populous state)

Area (Total Land and Water): 42,144 square miles (109,152 sq km), 36th-largest state

Largest City: Memphis, population 655,770

Nickname: The Volunteer State

Motto: Agriculture and Commerce

State Bird: Mockingbird

State Flower: Iris

State Mineral: Agate

State Tree: Tulip Poplar

State Songs: "My Homeland, Tennessee"; "When It's Iris Time In Tennessee"; "My Tennessee"; "Tennessee Waltz"; "Rocky Top"; "Tennessee" (1992); "The Pride of Tennessee"; "A Bicentennial Rap: 1796-1996"; "Smoky Mountain Rain"; "Tennessee" (2012)

Highest Point: Clingmans Dome, 6,643 feet (2,025 m)

Lowest Point: Mississippi River, 178 feet (54 m)

Average July High Temperature: 88°F (31°C)

Record High Temperature: 113°F (45°C), in Perryville on August 9, 1930

Average January Low Temperature: 27°F (-3°C)

Record Low Temperature: -32°F (-36°C), in Mountain City on December 30, 1917

Average Annual Precipitation: 53 inches (135 cm)

Number of U.S. Senators: 2

Number of U.S. Representatives: 9

U.S. Postal Service Abbreviation: TN

GEOGRAPHY

Tennessee is 432 miles (695 km) from east to west, but it is only 112 miles (180 km) from north to south. To the west are the states of Arkansas and Missouri, separated from Tennessee by the Mississippi River. Tennessee shares its southern border with three states: Mississippi, Alabama, and Georgia. To the east is North Carolina. To the north are Kentucky and Virginia.

Tennessee has three very unique regions. They are often called the "Grand Divisions." The regions include West, Middle, and East Tennessee.

West Tennessee is filled with lowlands, swamps, and river bottoms, with some rolling hills. These flood plains are sometimes called the Delta region. The fertile soil is good for growing crops, especially cotton.

Bald cypress trees grow in a Tennessee swamp.

Tennessee's total land and water area is 42,144 square miles (109,152 sq km). It is the 36th-largest state. The state capital is Nashville.

Middle Tennessee has flat land with some rolling hills. The soil is excellent for growing crops. There are many farms and manufacturing businesses in this region. The state capital of Nashville is in the north-central part of Middle Tennessee.

East Tennessee is filled with rugged mountains and hills. The Blue Ridge Mountains are in this region. They are part of the larger Appalachian Mountains, which run southwest to northeast along Tennessee's border with North Carolina. There are 15 mountains that rise above 6,000 feet (1,829 m). The highest point in the state is in this region. It is Clingmans Dome, which is in Great Smoky Mountains National Park. It soars 6,643 feet (2,025 m) above sea level.

Three major rivers are in Tennessee. The Mississippi River runs along the western state border. The Tennessee River begins near the city of Knoxville, in the east-central part of the state. It flows south into Alabama, and then loops back into Tennessee before exiting into Kentucky in the north. The Cumberland River loops into Tennessee from Kentucky, passing through the capital of Nashville.

The Tennessee Valley Authority (TVA) is a federal program that helped the state build large dams on its rivers starting in the 1930s. The dams controlled flooding. They also brought needed electricity to rural areas. The dams created many large reservoirs, which are enjoyed by boaters and anglers.

Tennessee's largest natural body of water is Reelfoot Lake, in the northwestern corner of the state. It was created by the New Madrid Earthquakes of 1811 and 1812. The earthquakes shook the ground so hard it sank, allowing river water to fill the shallow basin.

Reelfoot Lake

CLIMATE AND
WEATHER

Most of Tennessee has a humid, subtropical climate. That means there are hot summers and mild winters. Moist, southerly winds from the Gulf of Mexico affect Tennessee's climate. Statewide, Tennessee receives about 53 inches (135 cm) of precipitation yearly.

The average high temperature in July is 88°F (31°C). Summer nights are warm and humid. The record high for the state occurred in the town of Perryville on August 9, 1930. On that day, the thermometer climbed to 113°F (45°C).

A rainbow forms after a summer rain in Chattanooga, Tennessee.

A man walks through a snowstorm in Nashville, Tennessee. Winters are usually mild in Tennessee, but the state does get some snow each year.

Winters are usually mild in Tennessee. The average January low temperature is 27°F (-3°C). In the western and central parts of the state, daytime winter temperatures often rise to 50°F (10°C). In the high elevations of the Appalachian Mountains, the thermometer can sink to well below 0°F (-18°C). The state's record low is -32°F (-36°C). It occurred on December 30, 1917, in the town of Mountain City. Western Tennessee averages 5 inches (13 cm) of snow each year. The mountains of eastern Tennessee get about 16 inches (41 cm) of snow.

Tennessee sometimes suffers through severe weather, including tornadoes. About 26 twisters strike the state each year.

PLANTS AND
ANIMALS

In the 1700s, Tennessee was almost entirely covered by forests. After hundreds of years of settlement and farming, about 52 percent of the state remains forested. That equals about 14 million acres (5.7 million ha).

Because Tennessee has such a varied landscape—from wet river bottoms to tall mountains—there are many kinds of trees and other plants growing in the state. There are almost 200 species of trees in Tennessee. In well-drained flat areas are ash, black oak, bur oak, hackberry, pecan, beech, black walnut, maple, and cottonwood trees. In the swampy areas of the western part of the state are bald cypress, black willow, sweet gum, and river birch trees. Growing on the eastern mountains are ash, loblolly pine, hickory, red maple, and shortleaf pine trees.

Many types of trees are found in the Great Smoky Mountains.

Tulip Poplar

Tennessee's official state tree is the tulip poplar. Used by early pioneers to build houses and barns, fast-growing tulip poplars are found throughout the state. In the spring, they produce tulip-shaped, green-and-yellow flowers.

Tennessee's state flower is the purple iris. The state wildflower is the purple passionflower. Other wildflowers found in Tennessee's forests and meadows include bleeding hearts, fire pinks, phlox, evening primrose, crimson clover, wild geranium, red trillium, and many others.

Purple Passionflower

Tennessee's forests, mountains, and plains are filled with many kinds of animals. The state's largest wild animals include white-tailed deer, coyotes, cougars, elk, wild hogs, and black bears. Smaller mammals include opossums, eastern cottontail rabbits, swamp rabbits, eastern gray squirrels, muskrats, fishers, weasels, striped skunks, bobcats, and bats. The official state animal of Tennessee is the raccoon. The southern flying squirrel has a loose fold of skin on each side of its body. When it extends its front legs, the skin tightens and acts as a sail, allowing the rodent to glide as it hops from tree to tree.

Raccoon

Hundreds of species of birds can be found soaring through Tennessee's skies. Many migrate from other states for the winter, while others live in Tennessee year-round. Waterbirds include geese, gulls, terns, swans, loons, egrets, herons, pelicans, sandpipers, and many species of ducks. In the state's forestlands and grasslands are bobwhites, hawks, eagles, owls, mourning doves, ruffed grouse, cuckoos, woodpeckers, crows, blue jays, chickadees, sparrows, goldfinches, robins, and cardinals. The mockingbird is the official state bird.

Eastern Box Turtle

Many kinds of amphibians and reptiles live in Tennessee, including spotted salamanders, common mudpuppies, green tree frogs, American toads, snapping turtles, green anoles, and broad-headed skinks. The eastern box turtle is the official state reptile. Great Smoky Mountains National Park is famous for its great variety of salamanders.

Snakes found slithering in Tennessee include garter snakes, king snakes, black racers, and watersnakes. There are several venomous snakes, including copperheads, timber rattlesnakes, and cottonmouths. All snakes help control populations of rodents and other pests.

Fish found splashing in Tennessee's rivers and lakes include black bass, pike, perch, trout, gar, sturgeon, paddlefish, sunfish, and crappies.

Black-Lipped Salamander

HISTORY

People arrived in the Tennessee area at least 12,000 years ago, and perhaps much earlier. These nomadic Paleo-Indians were the ancient ancestors of today's Native Americans. As time went by, they formed groups, or tribes, and lived in villages and learned to grow crops.

By the time European explorers first arrived in the 1500s, several Native American tribes lived in the Tennessee area. The most powerful were the Chickasaw in the west and the Cherokee in the east. Other tribes included the Quapaw, Shawnee, Yucki, and Koasati tribes.

Paleo-Indians lived in the Tennessee area for thousands of years. As time went by, they formed groups, or tribes, and lived in villages and learned to grow crops.

Spanish explorers meet with Tennessee Native Americans in the 1500s.

Spanish explorer Hernando de Soto was probably the first European to visit the Tennessee area. He and the men of his expedition explored the American southeast in search of gold, and arrived in Tennessee in 1540. Other explorers from Spain, France, and England soon followed.

In the 1600s and 1700s, both France and Great Britain struggled to control North American land that included Tennessee. After the French and Indian War (1754-1763), the British were victorious. The area of Tennessee became part of the British colony of North Carolina.

Slaves were forced to plant and harvest crops on Tennessee plantations.

Starting in the late 1760s and 1770s, settlers built forts that eventually became towns. After the Revolutionary War (1775-1783), North Carolina gave up its western lands, including Tennessee. In 1790, Tennessee became an official territory of the United States. Tennessee joined the Union as the 16th state in 1796.

Tennessee depended heavily on agriculture. Large farms called plantations grew tobacco and cotton. They used slave labor to make a bigger profit. Thousands of African slaves were brought to Tennessee to do the backbreaking work of planting and harvesting crops.

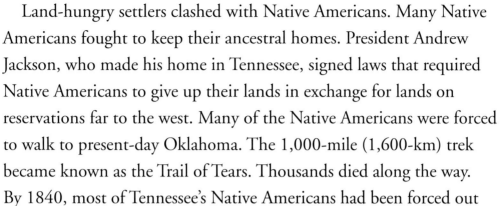

Land-hungry settlers clashed with Native Americans. Many Native Americans fought to keep their ancestral homes. President Andrew Jackson, who made his home in Tennessee, signed laws that required Native Americans to give up their lands in exchange for lands on reservations far to the west. Many of the Native Americans were forced to walk to present-day Oklahoma. The 1,000-mile (1,600-km) trek became known as the Trail of Tears. Thousands died along the way. By 1840, most of Tennessee's Native Americans had been forced out of the territory.

In the 1840s, railroads began to crisscross Tennessee. They brought people and products in and out of the state. More settlers poured into the area.

An 1885 train at a station in Chattanooga, Tennessee. During the 1800s, trains began to crisscross Tennessee.

Slavery divided the United States in the mid-1800s. Many people, especially in Northern states, wanted to end slavery. In 1861, Tennessee and 10 other Southern states seceded, or separated, from the United States. They formed a new country called the Confederate States of America.

The Civil War (1861-1865) between North and South caused much destruction in Tennessee. Hundreds of bloody battles were fought on the state's soil. The war also divided towns and families. Many people remained loyal to the Union. About 187,000 men fought for the Confederacy, but 51,000 took up arms for the Union. In 1865, the North won the war, and the slaves were freed.

After the war ended, there were tough times for the people of Tennessee. Many people were left homeless and without jobs. It took years to rebuild.

During World War I (1914-1918), Tennessee companies and farms helped with the war effort, which brought jobs to the state. However, in 1929, the Great Depression began. The nation's economy sank. The hard times lasted through most of the 1930s. Many people lost their jobs and homes.

World War I troops return home to friends and family in Memphis, Tennessee.

In 1933, the United States government started a corporation called the Tennessee Valley Authority (TVA). It helped develop resources in Tennessee and neighboring states. Large hydroelectric dams were built on Tennessee rivers, which brought electricity to poor rural areas. Many jobs came to Tennessee, and the state's economy was helped for decades.

Workers install a generator in the Norris Dam powerhouse. Norris Dam was the first major project of the Tennessee Valley Authority.

During World War II (1939-1945), the economy improved even more as Tennessee's factories and farms provided goods and food for the war effort. The United States government built Oak Ridge National Laboratory in the state. It was a scientific facility that helped develop the first atomic bombs.

Since the 1950s, many new businesses have moved to Tennessee. The state's economy has diversified. By 1980, less than six percent of Tennesseans made their living by farming. Manufacturing and service industries have increased, along with tourism.

DID YOU KNOW?

John Guwisguwi Ross was the principal chief of the Cherokee Nation from 1828-1866. He was educated and spoke English and Cherokee. Ross negotiated with leaders in Washington, DC, but eventually was forced to relocate his people to Oklahoma.

• The Cherokee were one of the largest Native American tribes of the American Southeast. Many Cherokee lived in present-day Tennessee. They were usually peaceful to American settlers. They adopted some of the culture of the newcomers. Some Cherokee became farmers, using the methods of the white settlers. Others dressed in European-style clothing and took jobs in white towns. A Cherokee man named Sequoyah created an alphabet in their native language. Many Cherokee were more literate than their white neighbors. In 1838, the United States military forced Cherokee families to move to reservations in present-day Oklahoma. Of the thousands of men, women, and children who were forced to walk to Oklahoma, an estimated 4,000 died along the way. Today, the march is called the Trail of Tears.

• There are between 8,600-10,000 caves in Tennessee, the most of any state. Carved from limestone by thousands of years of water erosion, the caves are home to nearly 1,000 species of animals, including the rare, blind Tennessee cave crayfish. Most of Tennessee's caves are privately owned. The largest show cave is Cumberland Caverns, near McMinnville. Discovered in 1810, it has more than 32 miles (51 km) of subterranean passages that can be explored.

• Tennessee's capital, Nashville, is nicknamed "Music City U.S.A." Many country music acts record at studios in the city. Nashville is also home to the Grand Ole Opry. Founded in 1925, it is one of the longest-running radio shows in the United States. Top country bands regularly perform live shows at the Opry, including famous stars such as Dolly Parton, Garth Brooks, Carrie Underwood, Blake Shelton, and the Dixie Chicks.

DID YOU KNOW?

PEOPLE

Casey Jones (1863-1900) was a railroad engineer from Jackson, Tennessee. On April 30, 1900, he drove his passenger train, the *Cannonball Express*, through rural Mississippi. It was a dark night, and very foggy. He saw too late that there was a stalled freight train on the tracks ahead. Jones blew the train whistle to warn people. He slammed on the brakes. He told the others in the locomotive to jump off the train while he continued trying to slow it down. The *Cannonball Express* crashed into the other train, but by staying on board, Jones saved the lives of his passengers. Casey Jones was the only one who died in the crash. His heroism was made popular by a song, "The Ballad of Casey Jones."

Al Gore (1948-) was born in Washington, DC, while his father was a senator from Tennessee. He grew up to become a politician like his dad. He served in the House of Representatives, and was also elected as a senator for Tennessee. He was the vice president of the United States from 1993-2001. His push for awareness of global climate change earned him the Nobel Peace Prize in 2007.

Justin Timberlake (1981-) is a singer, songwriter, and actor. He was born in Memphis, Tennessee, and grew up in the state. He started his show business career by appearing on *The All-New Mickey Mouse Club*. He became a singing sensation in 1995 with the pop group NSYNC. His first solo album, *Justified*, was released in 2002. He has won nine Grammy Awards. He has also appeared in several films, including *The Social Network*.

Dolly Parton (1946-) is a country music legend. She was born and raised in the Great Smoky Mountains region of eastern Tennessee. She began her career as a child, composing music and singing on radio and television shows. She moved to Nashville at age 18. She gained millions of fans with her powerful singing voice and stage presence. She has won eight Grammy Awards and seven Academy of Country Music Awards. In 1999, she was inducted into the Country Music Hall of Fame.

Aretha Franklin (1942-) is nicknamed "The Queen of Soul." Born in Memphis, Tennessee, she began singing soul and blues music professionally in the early 1960s. She rocketed to stardom with such classics as "Respect" and "Think." Franklin has won 18 Grammy Awards. In 1987, she became the first female performer inducted into the Rock and Roll Hall of Fame. In 2009, she sang at the inauguration of President Barack Obama.

Davy Crockett (1786-1836) was a legendary frontiersman and American folk hero. He was born in Greene County, on the eastern edge of Tennessee. He is often nicknamed "The King of the Wild Frontier." He was a skilled woodsman and sharpshooter. He was also a politician. Crockett represented Tennessee in the United States House of Representatives. He died in Texas at the Battle of the Alamo in 1836.

Jack Hanna (1947-) is a famous animal expert. He was born in Knoxville, Tennessee. He learned about animals while working on his father's farm and doing volunteer work for a veterinarian. After college, he opened a small pet store in Knoxville. He later went on to become the director of the Columbus Zoo and Aquarium in Columbus, Ohio. Hanna is most famous for his appearances with exotic animals on television shows such as *The Ellen DeGeneres Show* and *Good Morning America*.

CITIES

Nashville is the capital of Tennessee. It is the state's second-biggest city, with a population of 654,610. When all its surrounding suburbs and towns are counted, it is home to more than 1.7 million people. That makes it the biggest metropolitan area in the state. Located in north-central Tennessee, Nashville was settled in the 1770s as a port city on the Cumberland River. Today, it has many manufacturing businesses. Its economy also depends on health care, government, education, and the music industry. Its nickname is "Music City U.S.A." Nashville is also home to the world-famous Grand Ole Opry. Other must-see attractions include the Country Music Hall of Fame and Museum, the CMA Music Festival, and the Parthenon, a full-scale replica of the ancient columned structure in Athens, Greece.

Memphis is the largest city in Tennessee. Its population is 655,770. It is located in the southwestern corner of the state, along the Mississippi River. It is a busy shipping and railroad hub. There are also many manufacturing companies. The University of Memphis is just one of many colleges in the city. The National Civil Rights Museum marks the site where Martin Luther King Jr. was murdered in 1968. Beale Street, in downtown Memphis, is a popular destination for tourists. There are many blues nightclubs and restaurants. Pioneering blues musicians played in clubs on Beale Street in the late 1800s and early 1900s. At nearby Sun Studio, visitors can see where blues and rock legends, including Elvis Presley, recorded many of their hit records.

Knoxville is Tennessee's third-largest city. Its population is about 185,291. It is located in the east-central part of the state, along the Tennessee River. It was founded as a fort in 1786. Today, Knoxville is home to many manufacturing companies. Technology, finance, and education are also important. The University of Tennessee enrolls about 25,000 students yearly. Tourism gives a big boost to the city's economy. The World's Fair Park features the Sunsphere and Tennessee Amphitheater. Both were built for the 1982 World's Fair. Visitors can go to an observation deck at the Sunsphere for a 360-degree view of the city. Great Smoky Mountains National Park is nearby, along with other popular attractions such as Dollywood theme park.

Chattanooga is in the southeastern corner of Tennessee, near the Georgia border. It is the fourth-largest city in Tennessee. It has a population of 176,588. Chattanooga was settled by pioneers in the early 1800s. The city's unusual name was probably taken from the language of local Native Americans. It roughly means "rocky point." It refers to Lookout Mountain, which looms over the city on the southwestern side of the Tennessee River. Today, Chattanooga has a mix of service and manufacturing businesses. The city is also home to the Hunter Museum of American Art, the Chattanooga Theatre Centre, and the Chattanooga Symphony and Opera. The Tennessee Aquarium is one of the biggest aquariums in the nation. It features hundreds of freshwater and saltwater creatures, from playful river otters to tiger sharks.

TRANSPORTATION

Tennessee has 95,536 miles (153,750 km) of public roadways. Interstate I-40 is the main east-west road across the state. It connects the cities of Memphis, Nashville, and Knoxville. Interstates I-24 and I-65 are the main north-south routes through the state. Both pass through the capital of Nashville. I-75 goes north-south on the eastern side of the state, connecting Chattanooga with Knoxville.

Throughout much of its history, railroads have been an important way to move goods through Tennessee. Today, there are 25 freight railroads that haul products on 2,649 miles (4,263 km) of track. The most common goods hauled by rail include food products, chemicals, paper, farm products, and coal. Amtrak's City of New Orleans line whisks passengers from Memphis northward to the Kentucky border.

A CSX train hauls coal near Erwin, Tennessee.

Memphis International Airport opened in the early 1930s. Today, the busy airport sits on about 200 acres (81 ha) of land.

The International Port of Memphis is along the Mississippi River. It is the state's busiest port, and the fifth-largest inland port in the country. Many kinds of heavy, bulky cargo, such as grains and concrete, are loaded and unloaded from river barges. Nashville has a port along the Cumberland River. Chattanooga's port is on the Tennessee River.

Tennessee's busiest airports are in Nashville and Memphis. Nashville International Airport serves more than 11 million passengers yearly. Memphis International Airport handles about 3.8 million passengers yearly.

TRANSPORTATION

NATURAL RESOURCES

There are 67,300 farms in Tennessee. Most are small. The average size is just 162 acres (66 ha). In total, Tennessee farms occupy 10.9 million acres (4.4 million ha) of land. That is about 41 percent of the state's total land area.

The most valuable crops grown in Tennessee include corn for feeding livestock, hay, soybeans, cotton, beans, wheat, tobacco, squash, tomatoes, and apples. Soybeans are used for livestock feed, paints, and ink. Cotton fibers are used for clothing. Cotton seeds can be fed to cattle, or crushed to make oil. Cottonseed oil can be used for cooking, or for making soaps, plastics, and even medicines.

Cotton is bundled into plastic-covered 5,000-pound (2,300-kg) bales.

Tennessee farmers raise millions of broiler and egg-laying chickens.

Tennessee farmers raise more than 185 million broiler chickens each year. They also raise beef and dairy cattle, hogs, and egg-laying chickens.

Many minerals are found underground in Tennessee, especially in the eastern mountain areas. The state produces a small amount of high-quality coal. Other products mined include clay, sandstone, marble, crushed stone, zinc, plus sand and gravel.

Forests cover about half of Tennessee. The state harvests hardwoods, such as oak, yellow poplar, and hickory, plus softwoods such as pine and cedar. The wood is used to make flooring, cabinetry, paperboard, and other goods.

Several rivers in Tennessee are dammed to produce hydroelectric power. The Tennessee Valley Authority operates 19 hydroelectric dams in the state.

NATURAL RESOURCES

INDUSTRY

Until the mid-1900s, Tennessee was mainly an agricultural state. In the 1930s, the Great Depression hit the state's economy hard. The United States government formed a corporation called the Tennessee Valley Authority. It helped build dams along Tennessee's rivers to help stop flooding. The dams also produced electricity, which modernized rural areas. Tennessee was then able to attract more businesses.

Manufacturing accounts for about 10 percent of the state's employment. Tennessee factories produce chemicals, clothing, and industrial machinery. Other products include electronics, transportation equipment, processed food, beverages, and tobacco. Automobile manufacturing has been a top product in recent years. Nissan, General Motors, and Volkswagen all have large factories in the state.

Nissan Altimas are manufactured at the vehicle assembly plant in Smyrna, Tennessee.

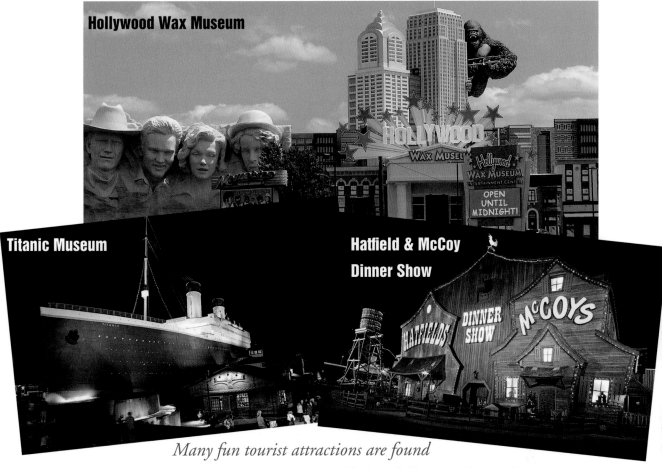

*Many fun tourist attractions are found
in Pigeon Forge, Tennessee. Tourism adds $18 billion to the state's economy.*

In recent decades, the service industry has become very important in Tennessee. Instead of making products, companies in the service industry sell services to other businesses and consumers. It includes businesses such as banking, financial services, health care, insurance, restaurants, and tourism. About 59 percent of Tennesseans are employed in the service industry.

Tourism is increasingly important to Tennessee. More than 101 million people visit the state each year. They are drawn by historic sites, the music industry, state parks, and Great Smoky Mountains National Park. Tourism adds almost $18 billion to the state economy each year, supporting more than 152,000 jobs.

SPORTS

Tennessee has three major league professional sports teams. The Tennessee Titans play in the National Football League (NFL). They play home games in Nashville. The Nashville Predators skate in the National Hockey League (NHL). The Memphis Grizzlies play in the National Basketball Association (NBA). There are also more than a dozen minor league teams in Tennessee representing baseball, ice hockey, and soccer.

High school and college sports are big in Tennessee. Vanderbilt University, in Nashville, usually has strong teams in men's and women's basketball and tennis. The University of Tennessee, in Knoxville, is known for its men's football team and its women's basketball team. The Tennessee Lady Volunteers basketball team has won eight National Collegiate Athletic Association (NCAA) Division I national championships.

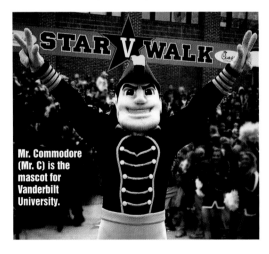

Mr. Commodore (Mr. C) is the mascot for Vanderbilt University.

Smokey is a mascot for the University of Tennessee.

A NASCAR race at the Bristol Motor Speedway track in Bristol, Tennessee. The track is a .533-mile (.86-km) concrete oval that first opened in 1961.

Auto racing is very popular in Tennessee. The Bristol Motor Speedway, in Bristol, Tennessee, is a NASCAR track that hosts many major races. It holds 160,000 racing fans, one of the biggest sports venues in the nation.

For outdoor lovers, Tennessee has many mountains and forests for hiking, hunting, or wildlife watching. Great Smoky Mountains National Park is the most-visited park in the nation. Cherokee National Forest is another popular spot. Tennessee has more than 50 state parks, wildlife refuges, and scenic rivers.

ENTERTAINMENT

There's one kind of entertainment that's never in short supply in Tennessee: music. Rural Appalachian folk music is often heard in the mountains of eastern Tennessee. Country western music and bluegrass are big in central Tennessee, especially in the Nashville area. Western Tennessee leans toward blues and rock-and-roll music.

In Memphis, visitors can tour Graceland, the former home of music

legend Elvis Presley. He died at the mansion in 1977, and was buried in a small cemetery on the grounds. Today, it is a National Historic Landmark, and a popular tourist attraction.

Graceland, Elvis Presley's home in Memphis, Tennessee, is visited by about 600,000 tourists each year.

Dollywood is a theme park featuring rides, crafts, and entertainment. The park opened in 1986 and today welcomes about 2.5 million guests each year.

Dollywood is a theme park located in Pigeon Forge, near Knoxville, in the shadow of the Great Smoky Mountains. Owned by country singer Dolly Parton, it is one of the most popular tourist attractions in the state. In addition to thrill rides, it features Appalachian music and crafts.

There are plenty of attractions in Tennessee for history lovers. The Hermitage, near Nashville, is the former home and plantation of President Andrew Jackson. Shiloh National Military Park, in southwestern Tennessee, preserves the site of the bloody, two-day Civil War battlefield. At the American Museum of Science & Energy, in Oak Ridge, visitors can learn about nuclear energy and the Manhattan Project, which helped develop the first atomic bombs.

ENTERTAINMENT

TIMELINE

10,000 BC—The first nomadic Paleo-Indians arrive in the present-day area of Tennessee.

1500s—Chickasaw, Cherokee, Quapaw, Shawnee, Yucki, and Koasati Native Americans settle in the Tennessee area.

1540—Spanish explorer Hernando de Soto explores the Tennessee area.

1763—England gains control of Tennessee.

1770s—Many settlers come to Tennessee.

1790—Tennessee becomes a territory of the United States.

1796—Tennessee becomes the 16th state in the Union.

1838—Native Americans are forced out of Tennessee on the Trail of Tears.

1861—Tennessee withdraws from the Union and joins the Confederate States of America. The Civil War begins.

1914-1918—World War I brings many jobs to Tennessee.

1925—The Grand Ole Opry begins broadcasting in Nashville, Tennessee.

1929—The Great Depression begins. Tennessee's economy is hit very hard.

1941-1945—America enters World War II. Oak Ridge National Laboratory is built in Tennessee.

1950s-1970s—New businesses move to Tennessee, creating a stronger economy.

1977—Elvis Presley dies at Graceland, his mansion, in Memphis, Tennessee.

2008—University of Tennessee Lady Vols win their 8th NCAA Women's Division I Basketball Championship.

2010—Spring flooding of the Cumberland River in Nashville forces many to evacuate. The Grand Ole Opry is heavily damaged, but quickly repaired.

2013—More than 9.4 million people visit Great Smoky Mountains National Park in eastern Tennessee, more than any other national park.

GLOSSARY

Alamo

A fort in San Antonio, Texas, where Mexican troops battled Americans fighting for Texas independence in 1836. Tennessee frontier legend Davy Crockett died during the battle.

Civil War

The war fought between America's Northern and Southern states from 1861-1865. The Southern states were for slavery. They wanted to start their own country. Northern states fought against slavery and a division of the country.

Confederacy

The Southern states of Alabama, Arkansas, Florida, Georgia, Louisiana, Mississippi, North Carolina, South Carolina, Tennessee, Texas, and Virginia. These states wanted to keep slavery legal. They broke away from the United States during the Civil War and formed their own country, known as the Confederate States of America, or the Confederacy. The Confederacy ended in 1865 when the war ended and the 11 Confederate states rejoined the U.S.

Elvis Presley

An American singer and actor known as the "King of Rock and Roll." He was born in Mississippi in 1935. He moved to Memphis, Tennessee, in 1948. He bought a mansion named Graceland, and lived there until his death in 1977.

Graceland

The former mansion and current burial place of Elvis Presley in Memphis. Today, it is a popular tourist attraction, hosting more than 600,000 visitors each year. It was declared a National Historic Landmark on March 27, 2006.

Great Depression

A time in American history beginning in 1929 and lasting for several years when many businesses failed and millions of people lost their jobs. The Great Depression hit Tennessee very hard.

NASCAR

National Association for Stock Car Auto Racing. NASCAR races are popular sporting events held across the United States. The Bristol Motor Speedway, in Bristol, Tennessee, hosts many NASCAR races.

New Madrid Earthquakes

A number of earthquakes that occurred in the New Madrid Seismic Zone in present-day Missouri, Arkansas, and Tennessee. Two very large quakes struck on December 16, 1811. Smaller aftershocks occurred in the weeks afterwards. A final mega-quake shook the area on February 7, 1812.

Tennessee Valley Authority

A corporation established by Congress in May 1933 to develop the Tennessee River area. Many jobs were created. Dams and hydroelectric power plants were built, electrical lines were laid, and other development occurred because of the TVA.

Trail of Tears

In the last years of the 1700s, land-hungry settlers began migrating westward. In 1838 and 1839, thousands of Cherokee, Creek, and other Native Americans were forced to move west to today's Oklahoma. Thousands died. Today, the brutal trek is called the Trail of Tears. The Native American land was turned over to plantation owners, who grew cotton and other cash crops. The plantations required many slaves to harvest the crops cheaply.

INDEX